Y. as Privilege:
anifesto

ard Phoenix

ROUGH TRADE BOOKS

"How do you start a band?"

I was 16, hanging around outside The Garage in Highbury & Islington in London, and I saw the drummer from the band I had come to watch, Idlewild. I started asking him a ton of questions, but the one that had been on my mind a lot at the time was, "How do you start a band?" He laughed and said, "just get some friends together and start a band."

All very straightforward it seemed. A couple of weeks later I rang up some friends, got them round my house where I had a drum kit, my brother's guitar and amp, some mics and a few other bits of gear, and I made us start a band—they were more interested in messing about, making food and drinking but I got us all to write some music, get some words together, record it on my tape player and there we had it—a band!

That band never rehearsed again, never played any gigs, never did anything, but that tape exists and is still a record of that time. This happened a few more times with a revolving door of people that weren't that interested, until I met some people that were. We started rehearsing regularly, we wrote our own songs, we bought better equipment, we started playing gigs, then booking our own gigs and inviting our friends to play too, we made flyers for the gigs, we started recording the songs we wrote, making demo-tapes, then making albums, working out how to create artwork, then making digital versions to send to pressing plants, learning what masters were, to also send off to the pressing plant to make our own records to sell at the gigs we were playing, buying a van, booking and going on tour—first in the UK, then we branched out into mainland Europe, Eastern Europe, Canada, Japan. We were trying to figure everything out as we went along, trying to write better songs, get better at our instruments, travel as much as we could, get better recordings, get better gigs and tours. This extended not only with regards to the band but also to each other—we met and started the band straightaway, we got to know each other through doing it and we ended up spending the majority of our time together. Before we had all met we had encountered the D.I.Y. ethos (Do-It-Yourself) through early punk bands like the Buzzcocks and more contemporary stuff (at the time) like Fugazi. This ethos can be boiled down to the idea that you don't need to wait for permission to do something creative, or share it with the world, you can just go and do it. If you want to start a band—you start a band, you want to play a gig—you book one yourself, you want to release a record—you press it yourself. It involves being motivated, organised and determined, but it makes anything possible.

I was in that band for eight years and I was learning the whole time, whether I knew it or not. I slowly realised I could turn what I had learnt into something more than what appeared on the surface. I started volunteering for an arts organisation called Carousel that worked with people with learning disabilities and after a couple of weeks I attended a club they organised where a couple of bands played that had members with learning disabilities: Beat Express and Heavy Load. Seeing these bands changed my life. It was the first time I had seen musicians with learning disabilities on stage performing and it was one of the best gigs I'd ever been to. I wondered why I hadn't heard of or seen these musicians play before. I thought that if I had enjoyed it so much, then other people would too. It also made me realise the opportunities I had as a musician weren't available to everyone.

D.I.Y. as Privilege – 13 point Manifesto for Musicians

1 See the privilege in being able to Do It Yourself.

2 Disabilities can be visible and invisible. Physical barriers and lack of understanding can exclude people. Think about how you can help remove barriers.

3 "Using privilege to dismantle privilege... one of the best ways to use your voice is to amplify voices that aren't being heard." - Rebecca Solnit

4 Do It Yourself can mean different things to different people and is a misleading term - it can mean you still work with people that record your music, people that make and sell your records, people that own the buildings you rehearse in, people that put on gigs, just as much as music facilitators, support workers or transport to and from a gig.

5 Be a supportive tool, be patient, listen, give people control.

6 "They're catching me on my weak points but not on my strong points." David M talking about Job Centre Plus. Catch people's strong points.

7 Don't assume what's accessible; ask and learn.

8 Disabled people performing at or attending gigs shouldn't be exceptional; the more it happens the more 'normal' it becomes. Make it the norm.

9 There is an audience for everything and ideas of what is 'good music' will always be political.

10 Everyone, regardless of their ability, can contribute to a music scene. Use existing support networks to get people on stage and in the audience - disability arts charities, organisations and support workers.

11 Turn up and keep turning up. Sometimes when supporting people being consistent is more impressive than being spectacular.

12 The more invisible you make yourself the more visible others will be.

13 Disabled people have senses of humour, laugh with people and enjoy yourself.

13
POINT
MANIFESTO
FOR
MUSICIANS

1

I started working with Beat Express not long after as a music facilitator, supporting their rehearsals, songwriting, recording and performances. The experience I had gained being in a band myself ended up being all the qualifications I needed to do it. I instantly fell in love with the work and was amazed that this could be a job.

For the band to rehearse, the organisation had a van which two of us would drive—we'd go to the offices, pick up all the gear we needed, then drive to where each of the members lived, pick them up, and then go to the rehearsal space. We'd then support them to set-up, making sure things were in tune, the keyboard worked, the drums were ready, the mics were plugged in and fully functioning. They would then practice their own songs, and Tom (who I was apprenticing for) and I would help however we were needed. For example if one of them needed notes taking down to help them remember their parts or if they needed to talk about writing new material, we'd be there to support them. Some of the members needed assistance conveying ideas, helping to get them out and to find middle-ground for all the band to be happy with the ideas for the song. We would help them write up the words, or form the riffs they wrote into structured songs, help the drummer perfect the beat he was trying or come up with something new if they wanted to.

It was a constant balancing act of trying to help fill the gaps in the band working together, but not imposing yourself too much on the process—sinking into the background when not needed, but being there if there were issues. It was super interesting and it didn't feel so different to the band I had been in previously—when it came down to it the only thing they didn't need much support with was the creative side of things. The openness to creativity the band had, the joy, positivity and love of performing was infectious.

While being a part of this process I came to the realisation that there were all these simple privileges that I was taking for granted in mine and my friends' ability to 'do it ourselves'. If we wanted to practice we could ring each other up, meet and hire a room together. But if we didn't have access to a phone, or we couldn't travel independently, didn't have direct access to our own money, access to instruments, or were even unable to communicate directly with one another and be understood, this apparently simple process couldn't happen.

2 There are many things that can stop us from taking part. When talking about disability and access the most obvious thing that comes to mind are ramps for a wheelchair user, so much so that the universal symbol for disability is someone using a wheelchair. Relating this to music, if there's no step-free access into a venue and somebody uses a wheelchair—audience member or performer—they can't get in.

However, when thinking more widely about the concept of disability, what is the thing that is preventing that person in a wheelchair from accessing the building? It's not the mobility issues that they might have, as the wheelchair is there to assist their movement. Rather, it is the absence of a suitable entrance that prevents (or disables) them from entering.

This, in a nutshell, is the Social Model of Disability—the idea that it is the environment, including the culture that surrounds us that can enable or disable us. The minds and bodies that belong to us, no matter how typical, common, ordinary or extraordinary, are the vessels in which we travel through the world, and if that world suits those minds and bodies better, and is designed for them, then it's a lot easier than when it isn't. When good design works you don't notice it, and this is one of the problems with noticing or accepting difference—if the world is designed for you then you don't notice that it's badly designed for others.

This isn't exclusive to physical environments by any means. Attitudes towards difference can exclude people.

There are many factors that can be taken for granted. The most basic premise of D.I.Y. being a privilege is that it can often simplify quite complex processes—physical, psychological and social. When I asked the drummer in Idlewild how to start a band and his response was to just go and do it, there was a permission given there that is sometimes all that is needed to support someone. There is also something in me having the confidence to ask that question, to think it was something I could do. As a white, neuro-typical, cis-gendered, straight, able-bodied man I saw myself reflected on stage whenever I went to gigs, so it wasn't a big leap of the imagination for me to imagine myself up there too. That permission to be on stage was given all the time by the images I saw in magazines, videos on TV, and the musicians I aspired to be like.

3

Touring was a really important part of the education I got in making and playing music. Meeting different people, encountering different cultures, understanding the world. I also learnt loads about music by watching other people that made music and the way they did it. Touring with a creative endeavour is something that can give you so much, without it being a controlled learning environment.

I was always a big advocate for touring, but I'd been told many times by various people that it was impossible to take musicians with learning disabilities on tour. The cost was too high, it was too much of a logistical nightmare, and there was no demand for it—people, I was told, wouldn't be interested.

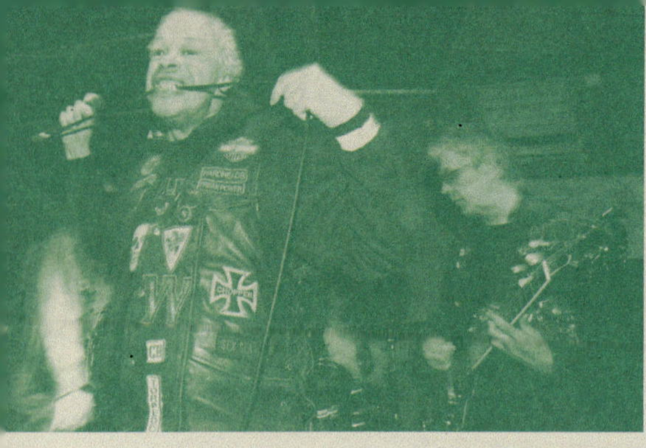

The man (left) with the microphone clenched between his teeth is called Kari, and the one with the guitar is called Pertti. They both played in a punk band called Pertti Kurikan Nimipäivät, or P.K.N. The other members were Sami who played bass and Toni who played drums. They live in Finland, and the photo is of them on stage at the Macbeth in Hoxton, playing London for the first time in 2013 on their first UK tour.

I founded my own one-person arts organisation, Constant Flux, and applied for £10,000 from Arts Council England to bring them over to do this tour with a metal band from the UK I had worked with in Brighton called Zombie Crash. I got the money. I roped in a lot of friends to help out, including Ben from Hard Skin to drive. I booked them gigs with D.I.Y. promoters in pubs, social centres and community venues that were accessible with local punk bands playing with them but also reached out to local disability organisations to bring in an audience that might not have come otherwise. The bands and audience reflected an inclusive, integrated space of disabled and non-disabled people. It was in turn one of the most ridiculous, life-affirming, organised and chaotic things I've ever done.

I recently read a tour diary from Pertti from this time, which was interesting as neither of us spoke each other's language, yet we had spent a whole week together. Below are some excerpts from Pertti's tour diary of the trip, translated from the Finnish.

WHARF CHAMBERS, LEEDS, 2 OCTOBER 2013

We were driving around. We ran an errand and went for a burger. Sami said that everyone takes care of their own business. Sami bought an english shirt. Kari said that's nothing for him. On the road we saw lovely and beautiful windmills and landscapes. Zombie Crash is a good band. The soundcheck was good. The toilet was in a condition... It wasn't cleaned. Smelled so much piss. Doesn't the english know that the piss needs to be cleaned. The english don't get it. All kinds of diseases comes. The gig went good. Went right. Then just hanging around drinking coke and coffee.

HEELEY SPORT AND SOCIAL CLUB, SHEFFIELD, 3 OCTOBER 2013
We went to Sheffield. The trip went fucking good. The store in Leeds was called Sami Hellenen. We saw a bloody hand ripped by a gigantic bear. It wasn't fun to watch. If you behave badly, you end up being ripped by a bear in the kingdom the bear. Ben asked if Pertti had done something bad. I have not. We did the soundcheck. Four bands were performing. Our performance was really fucking good. If Sami Helle says something, I can't play. And not when Toni is counting. We drove to the hotel. I got new friends. On the stage Smelled fart.

THE LEXINGTON, LONDON, 5 OCTOBER 2013
We went to drive towards the city. Three bands were performing. After the soundcheck we got food. PKN started to play rock. Then we came to Richards house to visit. Here we stay over the night. Tomorrow we eat breakfast. We hugged each other. Farewell as a memory.

4 "I'm emailing because Tom Cook and I have organised and set up a night for learning disabled musicians to perform live. We knew that a lot of the musicians we work with were getting frustrated at not getting to play as frequently as they'd like. We're doing this outside of any organisation, mainly because it isn't going to be possible to do it on the small scale that we think could work really well, and we want to see how it develops and grows by itself."

Below is a photo of the band Zombie Crash playing live, taken at the first edition of a night called *The Rock House*, originally based out of the Westhill Hall community centre in Brighton. It was set up by my long-time mentor Tom and myself in 2009. In an email sent out to our friends asking for their help in running it we included a short manifesto to explain our idea:

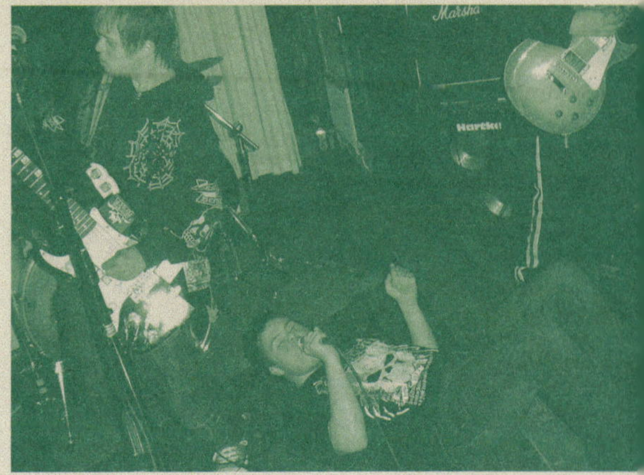

"A space for people with learning disabilities to develop and craft their live performance. Born out of a desire from musicians with learning disabilities to regularly play and perform in front of an audience in their hometown. A chance for these artists to create a unique community and music scene. A future aim is to run a separate integrated night but the focus is to provide as much stage time as possible for these new acts."

We didn't have the organisational capacity to support people outside of the night, all we could do was find a space for people to meet and play. The hall was really cheap to hire and included a PA, drum kit and amps and had flat access throughout. Tom and I would bring our guitars and keyboards and anything extra we might need. We'd make posters and flyers, we had a mailing list and an online presence. We made sure it was always on the third Tuesday of every month, so even if we were slack on keeping up on communication (which happened quite frequently) people would always know to show up. Everyone paid £2 to get in (including Tom and I) to cover costs and any profit we made was saved to pay for bands from further afield to travel to us. The policy for the first year was whoever showed up could play—whether they had a band or not. We dealt with all the logistics for the night to happen and for people to know it was happening, we just didn't work out the content. We trusted everyone that came to provide that.

Bands that we supported in our job would turn up, individuals that we supported in one-on-one sessions came, friends and family of band members showed up and played and as word spread we had people coming down that were just really into the music and the atmosphere of the night. Tom and I could play most instruments to support people and members from other bands were happy to fill in and improvise so we were never stuck for performances. The whole thing felt incredibly freeing for everyone involved. The audience in a way was not the priority, it was a sense of everyone doing something together.

The music played would vary wildly from act to act. Short sets were common, sometimes just one or two songs, and for the most part no-one really knew what was going to happen. After a while we started getting requests from people outside of our network to come and play, people that had formed bands with their support workers or friends just turned up and played, we also had people come down that wanted to join bands but didn't know how—here was a place people could meet, play together on the night and see where it went. People started burning CDs of their own music to sell and the audience grew. After five years at the Westhill Hall we started doing every other month at a larger venue in central Brighton, the Green Door Store. It was the move into creating integrated shows here, where bands with and without members with learning disabilities could all play together. The unknown improvised part of the night was still key (now known as The Rock House Band), but this time we roped in members of the guest bands, which was a way of drawing them into the culture and ethos of the night.

It happened every month, come rain or shine, except August when we had a break. There were nights when I couldn't have been more excited by doing it and there were some nights when it was the last thing I wanted to do. However, I always left feeling elated and that I was a part of something. In that room I saw and heard so many things that blew my mind and were unrepeatable. Due to distance and time, I slowly removed myself after eight years from The Rock House—even though I loved it, I knew it didn't need me to survive. In 2019, after 110 Rock Houses, it celebrated its 10th anniversary.

5

"The radical disability model says there is nothing wrong with any of us. To us, disability is not a point of individual or social tragedy but a natural and necessary part of human diversity. The tragedy of disability is not our minds and bodies but oppression, exclusion and marginalisation. We do not need to be cured. We do not need charity. We need respect, equality and access."

—A.J. Withers, *The Radical Model of Disability*

Without getting too philosophical, I think there's a big question as to why would you do this? Why would you recognise a privilege and give up power and control to others when doing so might not benefit you?

There is no straightforward answer to this and I think many people would see no reason to give up the power they have. For my part though, I have always felt slightly out of step with my surroundings, which in retrospect is probably why I am drawn to different forms of language and expression like art and music, and especially punk and D.I.Y.

Within the community and culture I get to support and be a part of I have benefitted massively from being in an environment that considers different ways of being in the world and ways of caring about people. By helping create an environment for others, I am also creating a space for myself. However, this can only happen by handing over control. I often feel most comfortable and cared for within these spaces and I believe my entire worldview is informed by them. Realising you can create your own versions of normality has been an incredibly liberating thing for me.

6 Charles Stuart is a musician and music facilitator with a very diverse CV, including working with people with learning disabilities, music in prisons and as Grace Jones' musical director. The story goes that one time during a break at work he was in the bathroom when he overheard someone talking to themselves in one of the stalls. There were multiple characters and voices, conversations and a storyline throughout the solo conversation. Charles was running a music session for young people with learning disabilities at creative arts company and charity Heart n Soul, and the only person that could've been having this conversation with themselves in the bathroom was one of the young people, Dean. This was really surprising though, as Dean was very quiet and hardly said anything at all in the sessions—it was thought for a while that he was non-verbal.

It turned out Dean pictures the world as if it were a TV show, taking things observed in his own life and twisting them into unique creations. Charles embraced Dean's world and helped magnify these creations, and they eventually formed a band alongside Dean's friend Mat called The Fish Police.

Dean was the front person for the band, the singer, the lyricist and the person that had the energy and charisma that held the whole thing together. At all of these things he excelled in a way I think a lot of people would not have guessed when first meeting him.

As well as the band, his imagination spawned a project called The Dean Rodney Singers, which brought to life Dean's world of mysterious creatures and superheroes living in a parallel universe. He worked with and visited seventy-two band members made up of musicians, singers and dancers from seven countries across the world—Japan, China, South Africa, Germany, Brazil, Croatia and the UK. In stark contrast to the scale of ambition and creativity he had when given the opportunity—at college they were giving him training in cleaning cars.

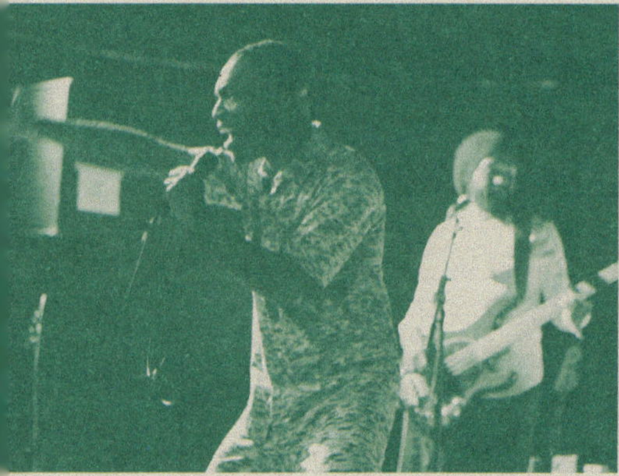

The photo to the left shows Dean performing with The Fish Police. Before the band parted ways they produced three EPs, their album *The Marzipan Transformations*, had been on tour all around the UK and travelled to Texas, New York and Indonesia. I have witnessed (on many occassions) their incredible ability to get audiences up dancing and singing along, even if they'd never heard them before. Dean is still very active, collaborating most recently with the band Ravioli Me Away on their wild and ambitious opera, *The View from Behind the Futuristic Rose Trellis* where he plays a god-like figure, and he is writing endless amounts of music, which my friend Lindsay said demonstrates his '25/7' work ethic.

7

"What do they have? The people you work with?"

This is a question I get asked a lot, as if a diagnosis or a word can encapsulate what it's like to spend time with someone. I don't expect these questions to be asked when I meet someone for the first time, more commonly I'd get "What do you do? What music do you like?" etc.

Unless someone tells me themselves, I have no idea what someone might be labelled as, I don't ever ask as it's not the way I want to think about people and for the most part there's no need for me to know. I recently had a great conversation about this with my friend Robyn Steward who I often work with, and I asked if I could share part of a talk she gave at D.I.Y. Space For London as part of a night of talks I organised and curated for the *In-Sight Weekend*—a collaboration with live music accessibility awareness organisation Attitude Is Everything:

"When I went to school I was in a mainstream school in primary, but I was in the 'special needs' class. That was really good because I've got all these disabilities, at that point I didn't even have the autism diagnosis, but I was with people with a mix of needs.

I learnt just from being in that environment that all kinds of things could happen, you just have to sort of roll with it. Sometimes I'll tell people about the people I was at school with and the kind of things that happened—they were things like people would smear poo on the walls and bite people's arms while they wrote, things like that. Sometimes I tell people, and once at a funding meeting I told someone and they went "Ohhh, did their cognitive impairment have an impact on your learning?"

And I'm like, I don't even think like that, y'know. So I reflected on what I said and realised I think it helped me to empathise with people, you know, understand other people even if at that point I wasn't really able to understand everything. I think what I learnt from those experiences was that everyone is different and people can behave in different ways, and surprising ways, and that the thing to do is find out from that person about what they need and their experiences, rather than being scared of it. I think that's what I learnt from it. [...]

What I'd like you to take away from this is that we really need to listen to each individual person and understand what they need because if we don't do that and we just make assumptions, then we won't be understanding that person, and sometimes a person might not be able to explain what their needs are so we might need to ask other people around that person."

8 I knew of Nani through going to and putting on punk shows but where I became friends with her was very different. She was known here as Maria, a teacher at Priory School in South London, a maintained Community Special School for students aged 11-19 with severe learning difficulties as well as students with neuro-diversities and on the Autistic Spectrum. She had heard that I supported people forming bands and because of her love of punk she wanted to help form one at the school. She got me in to meet the headteacher, Simon, and it turned out he played bass in a punk band in his youth so it wasn't a difficult sell and he agreed for the project to go ahead. Nani roped in Sam Truss, a teaching assistant that played guitar and had a group of students that showed interest in being in a band. Nani was a powerful force within the school, creating opportunities for her students that the education system didn't realise were possible. As she puts it in an article she wrote:

"Being part of a rock (or any other music style) band gives endless opportunities for learning, to develop skills and to grow as a person: a sense of belonging and developing relationships; self-esteem and confidence building; team work; creative and performing skills; risk-taking and learning by mistakes; literacy and communication skills; mathematical thinking and problem solving; money management; independence skills; and offers a fantastic opportunity to generalise skills."

Nani was also carving out space for herself, she saw it as an opportunity to learn with her students. She started learning the bass so she could support them, which eventually led to her long-held ambition of starting her first band. I saw Nani recently and she described the whole experience as a leveller, that she didn't feel like their teacher when playing and rehearsing together. I worked at the school for two years, helping to form the bands Rock Penguins and Diamond Glaze. Sam kept the project going and has helped a further two bands form at the school.

I think if you start a punk band at school it's rare you'll ever get an endorsement like this from your headteacher:

"What a revelation the first time I saw the band play to the whole school! Flashes of great bands from the Velvet Underground to the Vaccines were evident, but there was also an original and compelling sound with a hypnotic stage presence. It was one of the most moving experiences of my career."

9

"Every art-form is intimately related to a type of life experience. The difference between chamber music and jazz is not one of quality, finesse, or virtuosity but of two ways of life, which the people involved did not choose but were born into."

—John Berger

or Why I Love *Uptown Girl* by Westlife.

I met Jolene and her mum Pauline in Brighton through running a music-making course years ago. Jolene loves pop music, singing, and playing the guitar and wanted to do more music outside of the group sessions she was a part of. I wasn't a music teacher, music therapist, or anything like that, and it took a while to work out what we'd do in the sessions, but we knew when spending time with one another that music was the best way for us to communicate, so Jolene started coming round my house every Friday to make music. We messed around a lot and I recorded a lot of what we did, using music technology not only to broaden what we could do but also so we had a record of our time together. Something her and her mum could listen to when driving, or at home.

In the sessions she would sing, or play guitar or keyboard—whatever was to hand. We'd listen to music together and I would try and bring in elements of the songs she liked into the music we made. I would be experimenting with sounds and beats trying to determine what Jolene liked. I was aware that making loose, avant-garde, improvised music could work really well but that wasn't what Jolene listened to at all. Jolene had a speech therapist and we would integrate words she was using there into songs as well as using drawing to generate ideas.

We developed a routine before each session. She would arrive with her guitar on her back. I would greet her and her mum at the door. She'd come in, we'd take off the guitar together, which we'd put on a chair, and she'd take a seat on my sofa. I would then offer her a drink, she'd reply, "Tea please" (tea was a regular theme in her songs) and I'd pop off to the kitchen to make tea. When I'd return

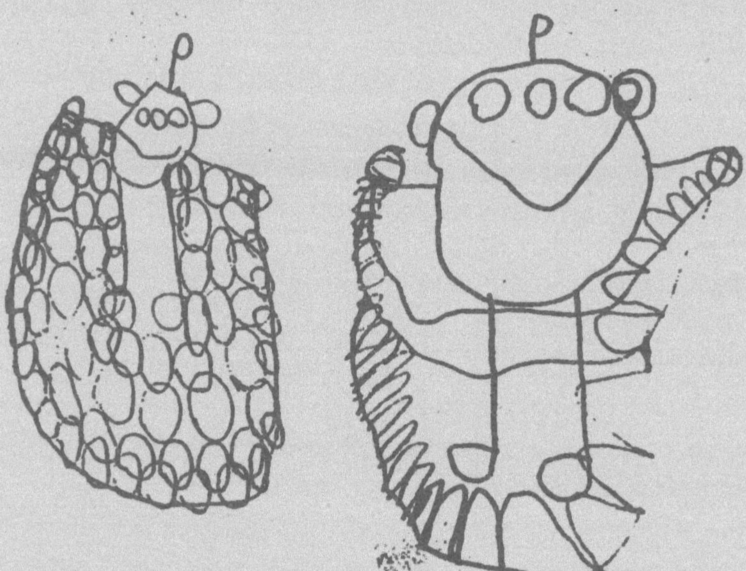

I'd ask if she wanted to listen to some music while we drank our tea. The first few weeks the choices varied until she settled on *Uptown Girl*, a cover of the Billy Joel song by the Irish boy band Westlife. We'd sit there and sing along to it, get warmed up and relaxed for whatever we did next.

I used to have an opinion on the 'quality' of the song, even in comparison to the original, ways of talking about the production of it, the context, the people singing on it, the people releasing it, but as I sat there week after week with Jolene drinking tea and singing along to Westlife, I began to care less and less about any of that stuff. I didn't know how it had come into Jolene's life or how it became so important to her, we didn't have those conversations—even if we could have it would've missed the point. Now when I hear that song, I'm *so* into it and I sing along as I know all the words. This has happened so much over the years now, that any resemblance of a well-curated taste in music has completely gone and I really don't care.

I think the realisation of the privileges I had made me re-evaluate my ability to reject mainstream culture and helped me question all the anger, frustration and despair I encountered through punk music—especially punk's nihilistic side. I think I concluded that the ability to say no and to reject mainstream culture often means that you have access to, or the ability to create your own subculture or scene. If you don't have that ability or choice, then how do you or why would you say no to what surrounds you?

I think the emotional connections we make to music and through music are sometimes under-valued. I developed a love of pop music through spending time with people that love pop music. I am fascinated by how songs travel and communicate so far and wide and how they can still be deemed 'bad music'. I realised the most important thing I could do with Jolene was to support her to create pop songs, filtered through her and me and the way we both played. I think we managed it and I still listen to the album we made to this day (and Westlife obviously).

10 Daniel Wakeford is probably the most well-known artist from the scene that I was a part of in Brighton. He became a TV star through a show on Channel 4 about dating. His innately wonderful personality shone through and people connected with him. Little did they know that for eight years he was going over to a house in Brighton every other Friday with lyrics he'd written, where he and Tom Cook would record a song in an hour, then every month perform them at The Rock House. The first song he ever wrote was called *The Black Of Lonely* and is one of the best songs I've ever heard.

From the first time I met him he always introduced himself as a pop star, every time he was on stage he performed like he was at Wembley Stadium, even in sound-checks. A while ago I saw him headline in London to a sold-out audience who were singing along to every word—he was performing the same as he always has, it's just the audience has finally caught up. The background of this growth is a whole load of people who had an innate belief in him and created opportunities for him to create and share his music—his parents, Tom, myself, Carousel in Brighton, Katie (his manager and bass player), his fans, his friends, his band, his support workers. Daniel just kept being Daniel, writing songs, recording, making intricate plans for new albums, singles, tours, bands, usually a couple of years ahead of everyone else. The TV show he was on finally let on that he was a musician and it blew up for him, with his music reaching its intended audience, and he was able to play in front of hundreds of people that loved him all around the country.

Daniel and his parents—who like many parents I've met through this work are just incredible—get recognised everywhere they go. He is a celebrity and a pop star... but he still goes to every Rock House, is down the front supporting the bands, his friends, and the scene he has helped build.

11

"I'm so glad I ventured into Croydon for the band all those years ago with James. His life changed considerably because of this and has indeed empowered him."
—Victoria Hicks, mother of James from The Carbonators

I've spent a lot of time in rooms with people making music and art, figuring out how to create things, what people want to make, how to work together, why we were even there. I've been in those rooms every Monday night for three years, every Friday night for two years, every third Tuesday night of the month for eight years, every second Saturday of the month for seven years, foregoing other things, not going out the night before to make sure I'm actually present the next day. These lengths of time expand and contract with importance. Sometimes it's because I love it, sometimes I'm there out of financial necessity, sometimes it's life-affirming, sometimes it's fine, sometimes it's easy, sometimes it's difficult, sometimes it's bad.

Below is a photo of The Carbonators from Croydon, playing at Power Lunches in Dalston. They are a band I supported for a number of years, initially travelling up from Brighton every week and then down from North London for rehearsals. The

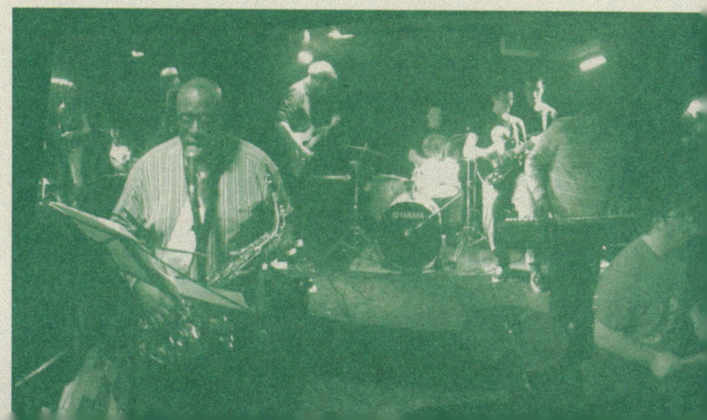

band formed so they could perform an hour-long improvisation with Damo Suzuki from CAN. We had two drummers, two saxophonists, a keyboard player that loved to get stuck on one chord, a guitar player, and I was playing bass—the instrument I could play with the least confidence. The gig went surprisingly well, finishing when Richard, one of the drummers, received a phone call from his wife on stage, which he dutifully answered, signalling the end of our set. We all got on and there was a bit of money from Club Soda who set up the gig to keep it going so we just kept meeting up. We ended up recording three albums together, *Beans, Super Sonic* and *Number One,* setting up a night in Croydon, and playing gigs all over the place. It wasn't the easiest band to get together or keep together, but when it worked it was glorious.

I often kept in the back of my mind the choice I had whether or not to be there though. For a lot of people I've met that choice isn't always theirs, so many other people are involved in their lives that can affect whether they can make it into that room— support staff, carers, personal assistants, family. Support staff often change—very frequently too—it is a job after all, which can change no matter what your emotional attachment is to them.

I'm extremely lucky that the job I've carved out for myself is creative, however, whenever people ask me about how to get into this work, or how I got into it, my main piece of advice is: just turn up.

12

The first instrument I started to play was the drums and as a drummer I learnt to inhabit the in-between space of hiding in the background. Of supporting the whole, but also being an essential part of the band. Being inconspicuous and important at the same time.

One of my favourite drummers of all time is Tommy Ramone, the original drummer from the Ramones. He just played for the song, providing the bare minimum for the song to exist, but for me that's what makes those early records so brilliant. He was their manager and producer and only played the drums because no one else wanted to and could actually keep up.

Despite this apparent background role, the drums can be loud and often impossible not to notice. The drums are full of contradictions—there are a million jokes about drummers, but drummers don't sit on a stool—drummers sit on a *throne*.

Many years ago I met four people called William, Sam, Alicia and Ehima at a project for young people with learning disabilities in South East London. When I met them I had just started as a music facilitator at the project Do Your Own Thing, and I think the youngest, William, was about 11 or 12.

Each of them has a unique talent and energy that we saw develop once a month at Do Your Own Thing, There was William's sense of rhythm and love of bass. Sam's incredible ability to play Beethoven pieces note perfect from memory but also his love of noise, synths and weird sounds—he loves listening to hard house, techno, jungle and Celine Dion. Alicia's beautiful, unique and delicate voice, she's completely unfazed in any situation and loves photography, fashion and Alicia Keys. Ehima is the live wire, with unbounded energy, laughter—near constant laughter—and he loves rock music, leather, bandanas, studded gloves and his favourite band of all time is Kiss.

In late 2015, they formed a band called Electric Fire. The one big change from stuff I had done before was that the whole band was based around music technology, and in particular a program called Ableton Live. The idea was that the technology would support them to be able to play live, but would be flexible enough for them to have the freedom to play how they wanted, improvise and change things on the fly.

Over the years we have learnt a lot about how this can work, how to write songs, how to record the best way, how to produce the music, how to perform it live. I say *we* because prior to working with them I only knew a little about producing electronic music, which was good in that they were the experts in their own music and I had to put the work in to learn how best to make what they wanted a reality.

I worked with them in the studio and at gigs, supporting their music-making and helping solve any technical problems that came up, but I was never on stage with them. Me being on stage with a bunch of young people playing dance music would instantly make them look 100% less cool... however cool I think I am, I'm not as cool as them. I used to be by the stage worrying if things were working or not, but now I'm typically found in the crowd dancing. I realised after a while though that despite removing myself from their ability to play live I could still prevent them from doing so by not being available to support the technical set-up. I had learnt over the years that putting myself in the position of being indispensable could become a barrier for whatever the project or band was. If I wasn't available, nothing could happen. So we've brought in other people that have learnt the set-up, got to know them, and who are now as much a part of the band as I am. I feel like the whole process of working with them has been a slow removal of myself, which is sometimes difficult to think about, as I love them and their music *so* much. Ehima was even my best man when I got married.

Max Roach is another favourite drummer, but he could not be more opposite to Tommy Ramone. He collaborated throughout his career, expanded the idea of what the drums could do, experimented and put himself front and centre. He created movement around himself, interest, intrigue and through trust he could bring others into that circle—allowing the audience he had to experience music they might not normally have come into contact with. Making yourself ultra-visible can create bonds that can be used to bring others along with you. The hardest part is letting go, to then allow others to be front and centre.

13

"NO LEE!!!", I scream at him while he sits there and giggles.

"THE SG IS A SUPERIOR GUITAR TO THE TELECASTER BECAUSE IT IS MADE BY GIBSON AND HAS MORE SUSTAINABILITY!"

"A pint of Newton and Ridley is the best!"

"NO LEE!!!!!! A PINT OF NEWTON AND RIDLEY IS NOT THE BEST AS IT IS FROM THE ROVERS RETURN WHICH IS IN CORONATION STREET WHICH IS ON ITV, CLEARLY THE WORST OF ALL TV CHANNELS. THE BEST PINT IS A DELICIOUS PINT OF LUXFORD AND COPLEY FROM THE QUEEN VIC IN ALBERT SQUARE IN EASTENDERS, ON THE BBC THE BEST OF ALL TV CHANNELS BECAUSE IT IS COMPLETELY AD-FREE!"

"No Limit by 2 Unlimited is the best song to boogie to."

"NO LEE, We Call It Acieed BY D-MOB IS THE BEST SONG TO DANCE TO... CLEARLY!"

"You have a Stratocaster."

"NO LEE...

The first time I met Lee from Beat Express we talked about how I needed to buy my own guitar for when I play with them. He told me I was going to buy a vintage white Telecaster. I wasn't really interested in getting a Telecaster, wasn't really a fan of their heavy, boxy design and that they sounded quite jangly (I was a bit new to the guitar and didn't really know much then, to be honest I still don't now) also they were far too expensive. So I said I probably wasn't, he insisted I would, and I thought we could agree to disagree. A couple of weeks later my friend Burton rang me up because he'd seen a deep red Gibson Epiphone SG in the window of Cash Converters in Kemptown in Brighton for £120. That sounded good to me so I cycled down there first thing in the morning and handed over £120 to the person behind the counter. That week at Beat Express practice I brought in my new deep red Gibson Epiphone SG guitar for Lee, who I was excited to show as he knew more about guitars than me. I can't remember his reaction exactly, probably because it was hard to gauge, but it definitely wasn't what I expected and all I know is that not long after he started calling me 'Mr. Telecaster' and giving me pieces of paper that said 'Richard Phoenix is a Telecaster man'.

I realised I had disappointed him, but who was he to tell me what to buy? I am my own person and I can make my own choices, so I would reply, "No Lee, I own an SG." But he continued calling me Mr. Telecaster so I thought I'd elaborate as to why I have an

SG, "No Lee, I am Mr. SG because I own an SG, it has a thick sound, not like the thin sound of the Telecaster."

I also thought I owed him an explanation of why I bought the SG, so I told him the story of buying it, which he seemed happy with. The next week he'd ask me about it again and I repeated the story, he'd ask again the next week too so I would add more detail each time I told him. The 'Mr. Telecaster' thing carried on and he would elaborate on why I owned a Telecaster—an important one being because it has *sustainability* (back then I guessed he meant the ability to sustain notes, but now I like to think of it as a quality in and of its own). I knew SG guitars were able to sustain notes better than Telecasters so I challenged him, saying that the SG was renowned for its sustainability. He wouldn't relent though and I started to suspect Lee was having me on a bit, so I started elaborating more on why I owned an SG. I got more and more theatrical in my responses, one time I openly shouted my answer at him in the van, part joking and part frustrated. Sometimes it's comforting knowing the routine of what you'll say and sometimes it's maddening! I thought I might have crossed the line, but he was sat there smiling and laughing like I had never seen him do before, which set me and everyone else in the van off. From then on it was constant and this conversation just developed its own life, we called them 'incorrect statements' and basically anything Lee said that was good, we knew it wasn't and we'd have to work out the opposite of what he'd said to find out what was good so we could shout it back to him. Everyone in the band got in on it, and it was surreal, complex, hilarious, and quite hard to keep on top of at times. Lee started to bring the statements written down on little bits of paper and we'd have to correct them all in the van before setting off, having to read them out, shouting out the correct response and also writing it down underneath.

What really got me though was the first birthday I had after meeting Lee. We were pretty deep in all this and I got a card from him, but on the inside it said *Dear Mr. SG*. I cried. I felt like it was a confirmation that with the 'incorrect statements' he was absolutely having me on, was completely taking the piss out of me, and I couldn't have been happier.

I don't see Lee as often as I used to, but at the 10th anniversary of The Rock House last year we talked about how I got my SG.

D.I.Y.

Stands for 'Do-It-Yourself'. In music it promotes the idea that anyone is capable of becoming a musician and sharing their music. It empowers individuals and communities, encouraging alternative approaches when faced with obstacles to achieving their objectives.

DISABILITY

I use the social model of disability. The idea that it is the environment, society and culture that surrounds someone, that creates barriers and obstacles, which disables and excludes them.

PRIVILEGE

The idea that advantages are available only to certain people in society.

MANIFESTO

A text that promotes a new idea with ways for carrying out changes the author believes should be made.